Surprised

Julie Murray

Abdo
EMOTIONS
Kids

abdopublishing.com

Published by Abdo Kids, a division of ABDO, PO Box 398166, Minneapolis, Minnesota 55439.
Copyright © 2017 by Abdo Consulting Group, Inc. International copyrights reserved in all countries.
No part of this book may be reproduced in any form without written permission from the publisher.

Printed in the United States of America, North Mankato, Minnesota.

052016

092016

THIS BOOK CONTAINS
RECYCLED MATERIALS

Photo Credits: iStock, Shutterstock

Production Contributors: Teddy Borth, Jennie Forsberg, Grace Hansen

Design Contributors: Christina Doffing, Candice Keimig, Dorothy Toth

Cataloging-in-Publication Data

Names: Murray, Julie, author.

Title: Surprised / by Julie Murray.

Description: Minneapolis, MN : Abdo Kids, [2017] | Series: Emotions | Includes
    bibliographical references and index.

Identifiers: LCCN 2015959116 | ISBN 9781680805260 (lib. bdg.) |
    ISBN 9781680805826 (ebook) | ISBN 9781680806380 (Read-to-me ebook)

Subjects: LCSH: Surprise--Juvenile literature. | Emotions--Juvenile literature.

Classification: DDC 152.4--dc23

LC record available at http://lccn.loc.gov/2015959116

Table of Contents

Surprised

We can feel startled when we are surprised. It is an emotion.

4

Amy got flowers.

She is surprised.

Sam's eyes open wide. His forehead goes up. His mouth opens. He is surprised!

Anna is surprised. She was
not expecting a gift.

It is Kate's birthday.

Her friends plan a party.

It is a surprise party!

Tina is surprised to see her dad.

She thought he was at work.

Kyle got an A on his test.

He is surprised.

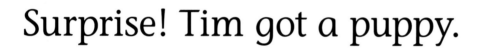

Surprise! Tim got a puppy.

When have you felt surprised?

21

Ways to Surprise Someone

do a chore without
being asked

help make breakfast
for everyone

draw a nice picture
for your teacher

surprise your friend
with a treat

Glossary

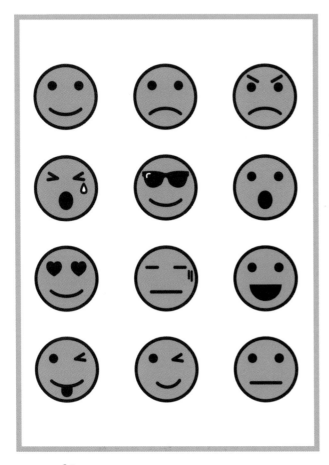

emotion
a strong feeling.

startled
surprised suddenly.

Index

abdokids.com

Use this code to log on to abdokids.com and access crafts, games, videos, and more!

Abdo Kids Code:
ESK5260